My First Maths

What Size Is It?

Jackie Walter

W

FRANKLIN WATTS

LONDON • SYDNEY

Notes for practitioners and parents

This series takes a fun, first look at maths in the environment around us.
What Size Is It? encourages children to look at how we measure different things,
for example length, weight, distance, height and time.
You could start by exploring different ways of measuring length and distance, using non standardised units,
such as hand spans, pencils, footsteps etc. You could also make estimates on weighing objects using
non standardised measures – the book weighs the same as six pens for example.
Begin a discussion on time by recalling the days of the week and the months of the year.
Do the children know when their birthday is? And how many years old will they be on their next birthday?

Franklin Watts
First published in Great Britain in 2016 by The Watts Publishing Group

Copyright © The Watts Publishing Group 2016

All rights reserved.

Credits
Series Editor: Jackie Hamley
Series Designer: Katie Bennett, Kreative Kupboard
Picture researcher: Diana Morris
Consultant: Kelvin Simms
Photo credits:
Africa Studio/Shutterstock: 3b, 11, 17l, 23br, 24tr.
Jaimie Duplass/Shutterstock: 23bl.
Everything/Shutterstock: 19tr, 24tcl.
Oliver Hoffmann/Shutterstock: 9t, 24cl.
James Jones Jr/Shutterstock: 13.
Kalumander/Shutterstock: 19br.
Monkey Business Images/Shutterstock: 21, 23tr.
NRT/Shutterstock: 9b, 24bl.
Elena Rudyk/Shutterstock: 2bl, 7.
Stickasa/Shutterstock: 2cr, 15.
swissmacky/Shutterstock: 5.
tanuha2001/Shutterstock: 3tl, 17r.
Richard Thomas/Dreamstime: front cover b.
Vicki Vale/Dreamstime: 14, 23tl, 24br.
Vitalinka/Shutterstock: front cover t, 1.

Voronin76/Shutterstock: 19bl, 24tl.
Rob Wilson/Shutterstock: 12, 24tc.
Phillip Yb Studio/Shutterstock: 3tr, 19tl.
Yongcharoen-kittiyaporn/Shutterstock: 2tl, 20, 24bc.

Every attempt has been made to clear copyright.
Should there be any inadvertent omission please apply to the publisher
for rectification.

Dewey number 516.1'5
ISBN 978 1 4451 4928 8

Printed in China

MIX
Paper from
responsible sources
FSC® C104740
www.fsc.org

Franklin Watts
An imprint of Hachette Children's Group, Part of The Watts Publishing
Group
Carmelite House, 50 Victoria Embankment, London EC4Y 0DZ
An Hachette UK Company
www.hachette.co.uk   www.franklinwatts.co.uk

Contents

What Size Is It?

We measure things to find out what size they are. There are lots of words to describe different sizes: tall or short; big or small; narrow or wide.

Can you think of any more words to describe size?

Different Sizes

These presents are different sizes.
The purple present is bigger than the
yellow present. The red present is smaller
than the blue present.

Is the purple present bigger or smaller
than the blue present?

Measuring Length

We can measure how long something is.
Which pencil is the longest?
Is the yellow pencil longer or shorter
than the orange pencil?

We can use a ruler to measure.
A ruler is marked with centimetres.
Centimetres are always the same length.

How many centimetres long is the blue pencil?

Measuring Height

We measure height in centimetres (cm) and metres (m).
There are 100 centimetres in a metre.

We can use a height chart or a tape
measure to measure height.

How tall are you?
Are you taller or shorter than your best friend?

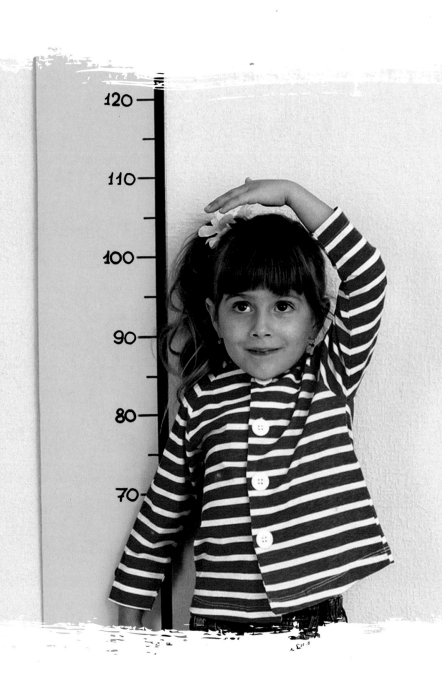

Measuring Distance and Speed

We can measure how far away something or somewhere is.

How far away is the airport?

We can measure speed, too.

How fast can you go on this road?

Measuring Weight

To measure how much something weighs,
we can use scales. Scales are marked in kilograms.

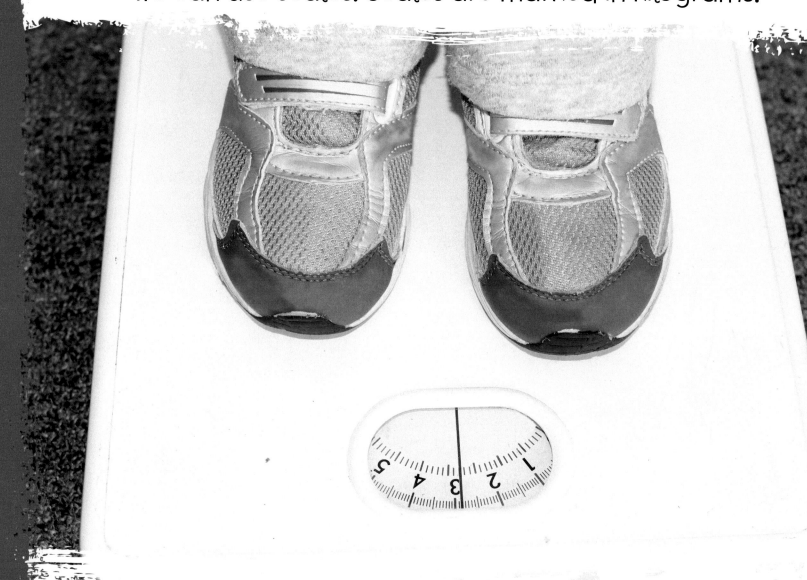

A kilogram is always the same weight.

How many kilograms do the strawberries weigh?

Do you weigh more or less than the strawberries?

Heavier or Lighter?

The pile of cushions is bigger than the pile of books.

Which pile do you think is heavier?

Which is lighter?

Measuring Liquid and Capacity

Liquid is measured in millilitres and litres.
Each of these bottles holds the same quantity of liquid, even though they are not the same shape.

The quantity of liquid that each bottle can hold is called its capacity. Whether the bottle is empty or full, it will still have the same capacity.

Measuring Time

We measure time in seconds, minutes and hours, and in days, weeks, months and years.

The red second hand takes one minute to go round the clock.

How many things can you do in one minute?

How long do you think it takes to put on your shoes?

Measure Yourself

We measure things in many ways, looking at their size, age, height, weight or capacity.

How many ways can you be measured?

23

Word Bank

capacity

distance

height

length

time

weight